AF487922
A Gift For:
From:
P

I Am Special

Devotionals for Every Season

For permissions or inquiries, please contact:
Liz A. Pitman, LLC
hello@lizpitman.com
petethepuzzlepiece.com

I Am Special: Devotionals for Every Season
ISBN: 979-8-9868889-9-6
First Edition: January 2026

Disclaimer:
This devotional is intended solely for educational and reflective purposes. It is not a substitute for professional advice or counseling.

The publisher and author disclaim any liability arising directly or indirectly from the use of this book.

Illustrated by Jane Brobst.

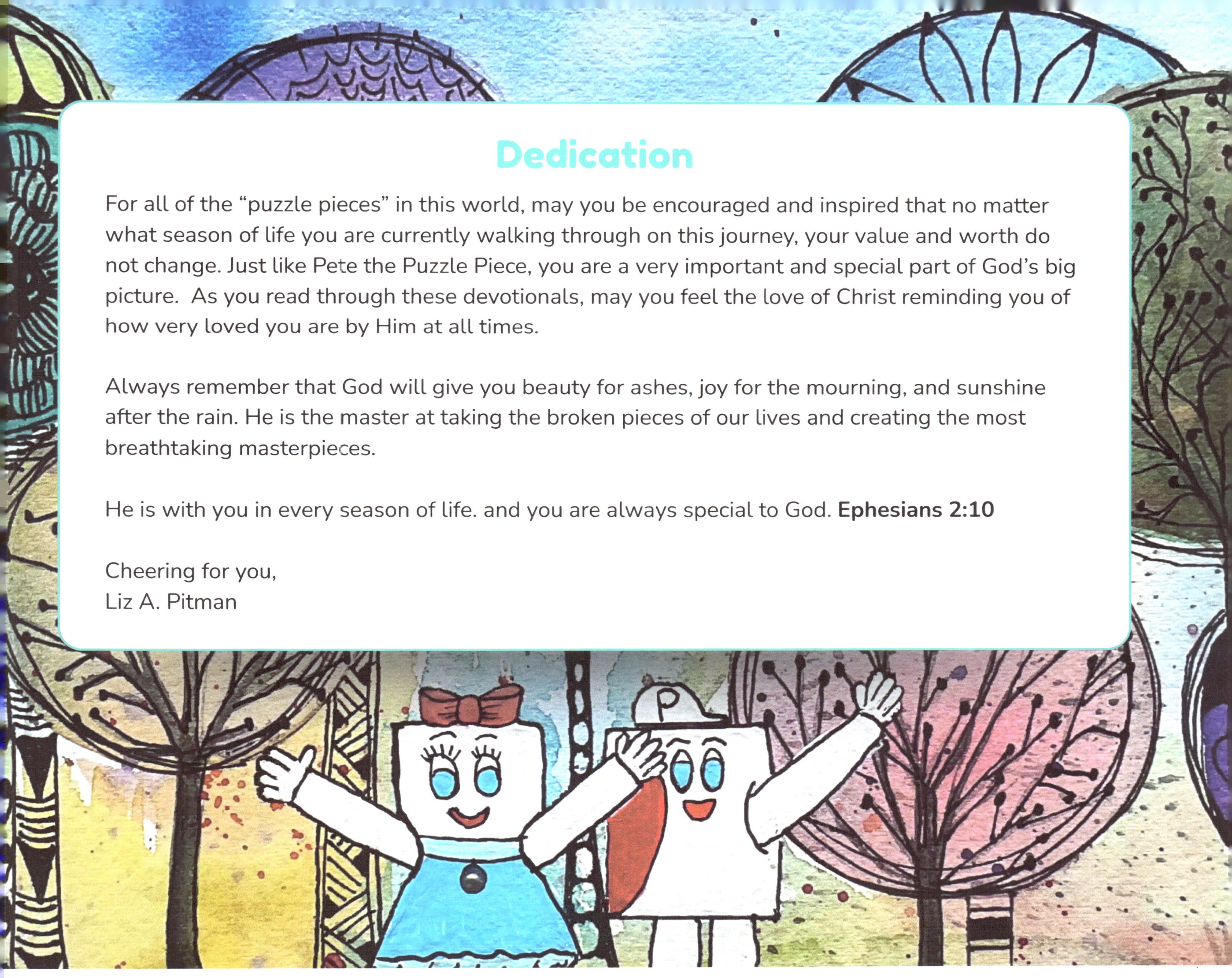

Dedication

For all of the "puzzle pieces" in this world, may you be encouraged and inspired that no matter what season of life you are currently walking through on this journey, your value and worth do not change. Just like Pete the Puzzle Piece, you are a very important and special part of God's big picture. As you read through these devotionals, may you feel the love of Christ reminding you of how very loved you are by Him at all times.

Always remember that God will give you beauty for ashes, joy for the mourning, and sunshine after the rain. He is the master at taking the broken pieces of our lives and creating the most breathtaking masterpieces.

He is with you in every season of life. and you are always special to God. **Ephesians 2:10**

Cheering for you,
Liz A. Pitman

New Beginnings

Pete the Puzzle Piece and his pal, Korbie the sheep, enjoy walking outside in the wintertime and watching the snow fall from the sky. They stand in amazement as they look at every snowflake, each unique and different made as a special creation from God.

As Pete and Korbie watch, they see that each individual snowflake comes together to form a layer of snow on the ground. That fresh blanket of crisp, fresh snow is a beautiful symbol of "New Beginnings" in Christ. Each day is a new beginning to remind yourself that you are fearfully and wonderfully made.

Just like that snowflake, you are one-of-a-kind, an incredible masterpiece made by the loving Heavenly Father. You make the world more special just because you are in it.

Activation:

Have you ever watched snow fall to the ground? Take the time to observe the beauty that is all around you. God is creative and loves to surprise us if we will just pay attention.

Scripture:
"For we are God's masterpiece. He has created us anew in Christ Jesus, so we can do the good things He planned for us long ago."

Ephesians 2:10 NLT

Winter Wonders

The beginning of a New Year is a wonderful time to pray and reflect on the amazing opportunities that are ahead. Pete and his pals spend quality moments together reading the Bible and writing down new goals and dreams for the upcoming year. They place the year in the Lord's hands and trust Him to guide their steps.

Pete encourages his pals to write down their goals in a journal. Examples of some of their goals would be: improving a skill this year, reading the Bible every day, being a good friend, etc…

They watch with wonder as they trust the Lord to lead their steps and light their paths throughout the year and on their next adventures.

Activation:

Just like Pete and his pals, spend time praying to the Lord and ask Him to show you His goals for your life in this new year. Write in a notebook or journal what God places on your heart as you trust Him with the plans He has for you. Then, ask the Lord to give you the strength to complete goals that He has shown you for this upcoming year.

Scripture:
"Then the LORD said to me, Write my answer plainly on tablets, so that a runner can carry the correct message to others. This vision is for a future time. It describes the end, and it will be fulfilled. If it seems slow in coming, wait patiently, for it will surely take place. It will not be delayed.'"

Habakkuk 2:2-3 NIV

Dream Big with Jesus

Dreams don't just take place when you sleep. They are desires that God places in your heart. What dream has God placed inside of you? What do you enjoy doing? What are your giftings that bring your heart joy?

Are you a singer like Sammy, an artist like Abby, an athlete like Bobby? Or, do you have other giftings like Pete the Puzzle Piece?

Don't be afraid to dream big with Jesus. He is able to accomplish more in your life than you can ask, think, or imagine.

Activation:

Spend time at the beginning of this new year reflecting on the giftings God has given you. Like Pete and his pals, write down your dreams and giftings and ask the Lord to use them for His glory and for His purposes. When you give the Lord what's in your hands, He can multiply your gifts and the dreams He has put inside of you to share His love with the world around you.

Scripture:
Read 1 Corinthians 12 aloud. Ask a trusted adult to explain the meaning of that passage and how it shows how important you are in God's big picture.

1 Corinthians 12

P
FA LA LA LA LA

Happy Heart's Day

Every year, Pete the Puzzle Piece and his pals celebrate a time that Pete calls "Happy Heart's Day". On this day, each puzzle piece gathers around and shares what makes each pal special. They recognize that every piece is needed because the Creator of the universe makes each one on purpose for a purpose.

A "light bulb" moment happened when Pete understood the love of Jesus and that he is God's special creation. Now, Pete can fully receive encouragement from others. Just like Pete, you can always feel special knowing that God loves you every second, every minute, every hour; every moment of the day. There is not a time that goes by that the Heavenly Father is not thinking about you. This should make your heart feel incredibly happy, too! You are forever loved by the God of the universe.

Activation:

During this time of year, take time to speak words of encouragement to others, whether it be through a compliment or whether you write a kind note to brighten someone else's day. Ask God to show you those that need to be lifted up on this "Happy Heart's Day", and remind them how very important they are in God's big picture.

Scripture:

"For God so loved the world that He gave His only Son. Whoever puts his trust in God's Son will not be lost but will have life that lasts forever."

John 3:16 NLT

You've Got a Friend in God

Do you know that God loves you so much and wants to spend time with you? No matter the season of life that you are in, whether you are happy or sad, lonely, or have lots of friends, God's love is always there, and He wants to be your friend.

You can trust God to listen to your prayers, your worries, your frustrations, and everything that concerns you. Unlike others who may be with you in one season and not the next, God is always there and available to talk to you.

Have you talked to God recently? He wants to hear from you! Today is a great day to start having a close friendship with God. He is the best friend you and I will ever have.

Activation:

In a notebook or journal, put the date on the top of the page, and write down prayer requests to the Lord. When you have an answer to prayer, make sure to record it in your prayer journal. God's timing in answering prayers can be immediate, not yet, or better than our actual prayers. He works in mysterious ways, and His ways are higher than ours. A prayer journal encourages your faith as you see God's faithfulness in your life and rely on Him as a trusted friend.

Scripture:
"When they call on me, I will answer; I will be with them in trouble. I will rescue and honor them."

Psalm 91:15 NLT

A True Friend Sticks Closer Than a Brother

Are you a good friend to others? Pete the Puzzle Piece learned on his journey of discovering his purpose that being a good friend involves realizing not only that He is special but that those around him are also special.

What are some words that come to mind when you think of "a good friend"? Friendly? Honest? Kind?... The Bible gives a great example of friendship between David and Jonathan. Although Jonathan was a prince, he looked out for his friend, David, who would become the future king of Israel. Jonathan could have been jealous of David since David would be taking the throne instead of Jonathan. However, Jonathan decided to cheer him on in the purposes that God had for David's life. They had a God ordained friendship that continues to inspire us today in our friendships with others.

You can be a good friend to someone, too!

Scripture:

"..., but a real friend sticks closer than a brother."

Proverbs 18:24b NLT

Activation:

In your notebook, write down five qualities of a good friend (ex. kindness, loyalty, trustworthy, etc...) Ask yourself if there are areas you need to improve as a friend? Which have you been strong in showing to others? Ask the Lord to help you work on the areas you need to improve and for Him to continue to help you be consistent in your strengths. Keep up the great work!

Spring Into Your Purpose

Spring is a wonderful time to celebrate the Risen King, Jesus. As the birds chirp and the flowers begin to bloom, hope comes alive and reminds us all that we can have hope because Jesus is alive. Pete the Puzzle Piece enjoys walking outside and seeing signs in God's creation that hope is in bloom.

He remembers that his heart is complete because of Jesus' sacrifice on the cross to forgive us of our sins, and His resurrection which gives us all an opportunity to receive the greatest gift, Jesus, into our hearts so that we spend eternity in Heaven. Have you asked Jesus to be your Lord and Savior?

If you are ready, today is a great day to make that decision!

Activation and Prayer:

If you are ready to ask Jesus to come into your heart, you can pray this prayer.

Dear Jesus,
Thank you for your sacrifice on the cross. Please forgive me for my sins and make my heart clean. I believe you died on the cross and rose again so that I can live forever with you in Heaven. I receive you as my Lord and Savior, Jesus. Amen

(Note: If you prayed this prayer, our team would love to hear this great news. With parental or guardian permission, email and let us know at hello@lizpitman.com.)

Scripture:

"If you declare with your mouth, 'Jesus is Lord,' and believe in your heart that God raised Him from the dead, you will be saved."

Romans 10:9 NIV

Watch for God's Miracles

Have you ever heard the phrase, "Don't cut down trees in the winter months?" During the winter, it is easy to look at trees without their leaves and consider them lifeless and without hope. However, underneath the ground their roots are still providing them food, and they are very much alive.

In life, circumstances can look very bad and beyond repair. Like leafless trees in winter, it is easy to get sad in situations where things look hopeless. Pete the Puzzle Piece loves to remind his pals not to give up in the hard times, because God's miracles can be right around the corner. The beginning of spring is a wonderful time to watch for God's miracles. New leaves begin to sprout on trees, reminding all of us that what we once considered barren or lifeless, is still very much alive underneath the surface.

God loves to use nature to remind us to hope in Him no matter the season of life that we are in at the moment. The Lord can shift our challenges or sad times and make them beautiful again.

Activation:

Ask a parent or guardian to take you on a walk outside. Notice the trees that are beginning to get their leaves back on their limbs after the wintertime. Take time to thank the Lord that just like those trees, dark or hopeless times can spring to life as we watch God work miracles in our circumstances.

Believe God's Promises

What is a promise? If you don't know what a promise is, ask your parent or guardian, to look up the definition with you, and read it out loud.

Man may break promises. It hurts when that happens. Sometimes, friends you trust let you down. At times, grown-ups can also let you down. Mankind is not perfect and when that happens it can really hurt and make trusting others hard.

The good news is that God never breaks His promises! The Bible is full of promises, and you can know with your whole heart that when God makes a promise to you, He keeps them 100% of the time. You can actually rest on the promises of God knowing that the promises He has spoken over your life will be fulfilled. One amazing promise in Scripture is found in **Deuteronomy 31:6** which says,

"Do not be afraid and do not panic before them. For the Lord your God will personally go ahead of you. He will neither fail you nor abandon you."

Wow! How encouraging! God says in His Word that He will always be there for us. No matter what friend or loved one may no longer be with us, God is always there. May this encourage your heart today and inspire you to find promises from God in Scripture that you can hold in your heart each and every day.

Scripture:

"God is not human, that He should lie, not a human being, that He should change His mind. Does He speak and then not act? Does He promise and not fulfill?"

Numbers 23:19-20 NIV

Activation:

Write these promises of God found in Scripture in your notebook or journal: **Proverbs 3:5-6, John 3:16, Jeremiah 29:11-13; Psalm 139:17-19.**

You can add on to the ones listed. As you find the promises in the Bible, think of it like a treasure hunt. Write them down, believe that God speaks these promises over your life, and hold on to these precious promises in your heart.

Showers of Blessing

Rain can be so refreshing! Pete the Puzzle Piece enjoys grabbing his umbrella with Abby the Artist when they hear or smell the sound of rain. Abby will listen to make sure there is no thunder or lightning and, if it is all clear, she will call out to Pete to join her. They stand amazed and watch the raindrops water the flowers and the grass. They also smile and remember that God sends rain to bring life to the dry places.

In the same way, God sends rain of refreshment through His Word. God refers to the Bible as "living water". It can bring hope to our hearts when we read it and can encourage us when we are weary. Even tiny raindrops are reminders that hope will bloom again.

Activation:

Look out the window when it is raining and watch the flowers and plants get fed. God sends the rain so that flowers will thrive. Remember as you watch that, although rain may fall in your life at times, God will use it for your spiritual growth.

Scripture:

"The rain and snow come down from the heavens and stay on the ground to water the earth. They cause the grain to grow, producing seed for the farmer and bread for the hungry. It is the same with My word. I send it out, and it always produces fruit. It will accomplish all I want it to, and it will prosper everywhere I send it."

Isaiah 55:10-11 NLT

April Showers Bring May Flowers

At times, rain may fall in our lives. The common phrase, "April showers bring May flowers", reminds us all that even when life feels stormy and gray, God is using it to make beautiful things. Flowers would not bloom without the rain. This phrase is a hope-filled reminder to look past the rain and realize it is bringing forth beauty.

Has it been symbolically "rainy" or "stormy" in your life lately? Things that are unexpected or hard can cause us to focus on the right here and now and not realize that as we trust the Lord, He can bring beauty out of the things we are going through during a rainy season.

Hold onto hope and know that God is working out all things for your good and for His glory.

Know that in due season, the "flowers" will bloom in your life, and beautiful things will begin to emerge from the "rainy" season you have experienced.

Activation:

Journal with the Lord and write down some areas that life can be "rainy" at the moment. List prayer requests next to those areas, and ask the Lord to help you trust Him to turn those hard situations around. As you see Him answer your prayers, write them down and praise the Lord for His goodness in your life.

Scripture:

"And we know that God causes everything to work together for the good of those who love God and are called according to His purpose for them."

Romans 8:28 NLT

God Collects Your Tears in a Bottle

Have you ever thought that when it rains, it looks like tears falling from the sky?... Did you know that there are happy tears and sad tears?... God gives us the ability to express our emotions, and tears can celebrate joy in our lives, or they can represent the pain or hurt that we are feeling.

Do you want to know something incredible?...

The Bible says that God collects our tears in a bottle. It also says that He records our tears in His book. He knows how many tears we shed and keeps track of each one! God cares so much about us! When you continue to do the right thing and help others even when you are sad, you are watering the soil in your own life. One day, you will reap a harvest for the amazing things that you do for the Lord even if it is during a "rainy or difficult" season in your own life!

How comforting to know that the God of the universe takes the time to notice every detail of our lives. He treasures us.

Activation:

The next time you are sad, ask the Lord to show you how to bring joy into the life of someone else. The Bible says that those who sow in tears will reap with shouts of joy. When you continue to encourage others and do what God asks you to do, even when you are hurting, God has ways to bring joy to your heart in ways that only He can.

Hope Blooms

The sweet smell of flowers rewards us all for enduring a rainy season. Pete the Puzzle Piece and his pals take time to sniff the flowers and look at the unique beauty in each one. God is so creative! Pete looks at all of the colors of each petal, the yellows, pinks, purples, and reds and appreciates how each adds so much variety to life. Like the colorful flowers, all of us are made with extraordinary qualities and distinctions. No matter our outward appearance or personality, we have a special place in this world that only we can fill.

That is why it is so important not to compare yourself to others. You are designed exactly the way you are to make a difference in this world. God makes you exactly the way you are for a reason. Each amazing quality and feature about you is made on purpose for a purpose.

The Creator makes all things by His beautiful design and handiwork.

Scripture:

"Thank you for making me so wonderfully complex! Your workmanship is marvelous—how well I know it."

Psalm 139:14 NLT

Activation:

Write down in your journal several qualities or characteristics that God has given to you. If you need help, ask a parent or guardian to share with you characters and qualities that they notice about you. Thank the Lord for making you unique and special.

Take Time to Sniff the Flowers

Do you have a favorite flower? Abby the Artist's favorite flower is the rose. Pete really likes lavender. With so many types and colors and scents, every person might have a different favorite. We all can admire the variety of creation in our own special way.

Life can get very busy sometimes...going from one activity to the next. It is easy to lose sight of the beauty around us and not pay attention to amazing things that can remind us that God is in the details. That is why Pete and his pals schedule an activity outside when the flowers bloom and have a picnic together to enjoy the world around them.

It is important to look up and appreciate the beauty of God's creation. Be intentional to observe and breathe in the wonderful things that the Lord has made.

Activation:

Take time out of the busyness of life, and ask a parent or guardian if they will walk with you outside or have a picnic outdoors. Bring your journal or notebook and draw flowers that you see around you. Ask them what type of flowers that you notice. If you have a favorite flower, write that down in your notebook.

(Note: Do not sniff flowers if you are allergic to them. Make sure to ask a parent or guardian just to be careful.)

Scripture:

"And if God cares so wonderfully for wildflowers that are here today and thrown into the fire tomorrow, He will certainly care for you. Why do you have so little faith?...Seek first the Kingdom of God above all else, and live righteously, and He will give you everything you need."

Matthew 6:30 & 33 NLT

God is the Master Gardener

Do you know someone who has a garden?...Maybe you have a vegetable garden, fruit garden, or a flower garden in your backyard. Sammy the Singer has a vegetable garden and brings fresh vegetables for his pals when they have a picnic. Sammy takes good care of his prized produce. His pals look forward to eating the vegetables and appreciate his hard work.

As a Master Gardener, God is very specific and makes beautiful gardens. In the same way, He pays very close attention to each of us. When we receive Him into our lives and draw water from His Word, He gives life and encouragement to us. Reading the Bible strengthens us to bear much fruit by how we act and talk with one another.

Activation:

With parental or guardian permission, ask if you can visit a garden. Maybe you can watch a gardener and learn how tend to their fruits, vegetables, or flowers. Notice how they take good care of what is entrusted to them. As you observe, know how much more God watches and takes good care of you.

Scripture:

"I am the true grapevine, and my Father is the gardener. He cuts off every branch of mine that doesn't produce fruit, and He prunes the branches that do bear fruit so they will produce even more..." Verse 5 also says, "Yes, I am the vine; you are the branches. Those who remain in Me, and I in them, will produce much fruit. For apart from Me you can do nothing."

John 15:1-2,5 NLT

Summer Days

What is your favorite season? Summer is one of Pete the Puzzle Piece's favorite seasons. He and his pals spend time at the beach building sandcastles, watching the waves, flying kites that soar to the heights, and admiring God beautiful handiwork at sunset. When God paints the sky every night, each stroke and color is different. Not one sunset is exactly alike.

Pete looks up at the sunset and likes to hear Abby the Artist talk about how the sky is like a big canvas and that God is the best artist that paints each sunset beautifully. In the same way, you are His masterpiece that He has created masterfully.

When we watch the sunset, what a wonderful reminder that God is creative and does all things well! He loves to paint beautiful sunsets for us to enjoy!

Activation:

Ask a parent or guardian to watch the sunset with you. Look at all of the colors. You could even color the sky in your notebook or journal. Remember to take time to look at the beautiful artwork that God paints.

Scripture:

"The heavens proclaim the glory of God. The skies display His craftsmanship."

Psalm 19:1 NLT

Enjoy the Little Things

God loves using little things to do big things. It can be easy to overlook things that are tiny. It is important to not pass over things that may seem small because they have the potential to do mighty things!

When Pete the Puzzle Piece goes into the forest, he likes to pick up an acorn. He reminds his pals that that one little acorn can produce a giant oak tree. Once an acorn goes underneath the ground, it cracks, and can then grow roots and sprout a ginormous tree! It's amazing that the Lord is able to take something so tiny and create something so large!

In Scripture, God took a tiny stone that David had in his hand and defeated a giant by His power. David obeyed and was willing to let the Lord use something small to accomplish Kingdom purposes . What abilities can you give to the Lord and have Him use for His glory? Even if you think it is something small, God can take your giftings and do something extraordinary with your life!

Scripture:

"Do not despise these small beginnings, for the LORD rejoices to see the work begin, to see the plumb line in Zerubbabel's hand."

Zechariah 4:10 NLT

Activation:

With parental or guardian permission, go on a walk and pick up an acorn. Look at how tiny it is. Find an oak tree and observe how massive it is compared to the acorn. In your journal or notebook, draw a picture of an acorn and an oak tree, and color your artwork.

Fruits of the Spirit

What is your favorite fruit? Grapes, cherries, oranges, pineapple, strawberries?...

Warm weather allows abundant fruit to grow. Fruit can be a refreshing treat after a day of playing in the sunshine. Pete loves to eat some pineapple while he plays on the beach.

When we follow Jesus, the Bible says that we should see the symbolic "fruit" of the Holy Spirit in our lives. It is called the "fruits of the Spirit".

Some "fruits of the Spirit" that are listed in Galatians are *love, joy, peace, patience, kindness, goodness, faithfulness, and self-control.* When we read the Bible, these "fruits" become more visible in how we treat others. We want to ask God to help us show sweet fruit and be honoring in the way that we live and show His love to those around us.

Activation:

Write in your journal the fruits of the Spirit listed here: *Love, Joy, Peace, Patience, Kindness, Goodness, Faithfulness, and Self-control.* Write down "fruits" that you need to work on and ask God how you can work on those areas. Write down the "fruits" that you are doing a wonderful job of showing to others.

Note: If you need help, ask a parent or guardian to help you name some "fruits" you can work on, and some you are doing a great job showing others. As works in progress, we always need the Lord's help.

Treasure
the Moment

Treasure the Memories

What do you think of when you hear the word "Valuable"?
Most people automatically think of things that are rare or shiny.
Things of value aren't just limited to jewels or money, they can also include memories in your treasure box with friends or loved ones.

Pete the Puzzle Piece loves to add memories in his treasure box by spending time with his pals. In the warmer months, Pete, Will, Bobo the dog, and his doggie friends enjoy the outdoors and walk with balloons that they buy at the carnival. As they walk home after a fun-filled day, they laugh and make memories together that will last a lifetime. When he gets back home, Pete loves to write these memories down in his journal. It reminds him of his adventures and special times with others.

Activation:
Write down some of your favorite memories. Why was it special?
What do you remember most?
What are some "treasure box" moments you would like to make this year?

As you make memories in your treasure box with your family and friends, make sure to write them down, so you can remember all the wonderful details in the future.

Scripture:
"This is the day the Lord has made. We will rejoice and be glad in it."

Psalm 118:24 NLT

Let God Carry It

Does life ever feel heavy? No matter the season, we all go through times where the cares of the world feel like weights on our shoulders. The good news is that we do not need to carry the weight of those worries by ourselves. When Pete and his pals walk home from the carnival with their balloons, they remind each other that balloons are able to float in the sky and appear almost weightless. They talk about how God takes those worries that can weigh them down and helps relieve the heaviness by carrying those concerns on His shoulders.

How do we allow God to take the burdens that pile up in our lives? The key word is *Trust*. When we trust that the Lord wants the best for us and that He can do the heavy lifting in our lives, we don't have to do everything in our own strength.

What a relief to know that the God of the universe is able to handle all of our problems, frustrations, and worries and take care of them on our behalf.

Activation:

Draw balloons in your journal. In each circle, list something that has been bothering you or causing you worry. Take those items in the balloon to prayer and watch God work on your behalf. As you feel the weight get lighter, color over the word with colored pencils, crayons, or markers as a reminder that God does the heavy lifting for you.

Scripture:

"Then Jesus said, 'Come to Me, all of you who are weary and carry heavy burdens, and I will give you rest.'"

Matthew 11:28 NLT

The Truth Will Set You Free

Have you ever compared yourself to others? Someone could have a similar gifting as yours like singing or sports or academics, etc...and you begin to wonder if your gifts are important in this world. Maybe someone has a totally different gift, and you wish you had what they had instead of your own. Pete the Puzzle Piece struggled with that until he realized that he had a very special place in the big picture.

When you compare, you rob yourself of the special calling that God has placed inside of you for a reason. The enemy can use others to make you feel less than or simply make you hard on yourself, and you can begin to question what you are even good at doing.

Refuse to listen to the lies that someone else could do the job better and that your gifts aren't valuable. Whatever dreams God has placed inside of your heart are there for a reason. No one else can replace your purpose. Your voice and your gift will reach others for Christ that no one else can.

Believe the truth of who God says you are: His incredible masterPIECE (Ephesians 2:10). This truth will set you free to do the amazing things that God has in store for your life.

Scripture:

"Bring all who claim Me as their God, for I have made them for My glory. It was I who created them."

Isaiah 43:7 NLT

Activation:

Ask yourself if you have been comparing yourself with others. Take time to reflect and focus on the truth of who God says you are. Pray and ask God to show you what you are gifted in doing. Work with excellence and continue to grow in those giftings as you ask God to empower you to share your giftings with the world.

Give God the Paint Brush

Abby the Artist can paint outside for hours and hours. Spending time outdoors around sunset is actually her favorite time to create artwork. She is known throughout the town of Jigsaw for her beautiful murals. One of her favorite things to capture is nature and the sky. Surrounded by the flowers and beauty of God's creation, she listens to the birds and gets caught up in the moment as she takes the paint and glides it across her canvas.

People from all over admire her artwork as she vividly draws the beautiful scenery of the town. When Abby takes the paint brush, she thinks about how God, the Master Artist, takes the brush in each of our lives and with each paint stroke creates a masterpiece.

The paint brush surrenders to the artist's hand and allows the paint and brush to coordinate with exact timing and precision to create a one-of-a-kind piece of art.

When we surrender or let God have control of our lives, He can create a beautiful work of art from our stories.

Scripture:
"He has made everything beautiful in its time."

Ecclesiastes 3:11 NLT

Activation:

With parental or guardian permission, paint a picture and ask if you can place it on the refrigerator or bathroom mirror. As you look at it, remind yourself that God is painting a beautiful picture with your life.

Be Still and Trust God

Take a deep breath.

Sometimes, the most trusting thing you can do, is to take a breath and rest knowing that God is in control. He holds the whole world in His hands. The Bible says in Job 12:10, *"In His hand is the life of every creature and the breath of all mankind."* (NIV) You don't have to handle everything in your own strength. God wants you to know that He cares about you so much that you can trust Him to hold your world and the things that are on your heart.

Abby the Artist spends time quietly painting and listening in the stillness to hear from the Lord. Many times, noise can distract us from hearing that still small voice of God where He gently leads and guides. When we breathe and get quiet before Him, He can reveal things to us and show us next steps in our journey with Him.

Activation:

Find your Bible, and spend time reading His Word. As you listen to God's voice, write down what He speaks to your heart and what He shows you in your time with Him.

Scripture:

"Be still, and know that I am God; I will be exalted among the nations, I will be exalted in the earth."

Psalm 46:10 NIV

With God All Things Are Possible

Have you ever heard someone say, "That's impossible."
Did you know that God is all-powerful and that with Him all things are possible?

The Heavenly Father is not limited by time or space. He can turn impossible situations around. Isaiah 55:8-9 says that God's ways are higher than our ways and that His thoughts are higher than our thoughts.

In the Bible, God performed many miracles that man would call "impossible". He caused the sun to stand still for Joshua, He strengthened Elijah to outrun a chariot, He parted the Red Sea for Moses, and He gave a child to Abraham and Sarah in their old age.

God still performs miracles today. Place those impossible situations in the Lord's hands and trust Him with the outcome.

Activation:

Write down circumstances that may seem impossible in your life. Pray over those circumstances and ask the Lord to have His way in each and every situation. Trust Him with the results.

God's Promises are "Yes" and "Amen"!

As the summer months begin to transition into fall, Izzy and Pete go on walks to watch the trees begin to change colors. Izzy particularly loves the yellow hues. Pete enjoys all of the colors on the trees.

As seasons change, it can create different emotions. Some love the warm seasons, while others love the cold seasons. God created everyone so differently to make life more interesting.

One thing is certain. No matter the season, God's promises are never changing. When He makes a promise, He keeps His Word. It says in the Bible that God's promises are "Yes" and "Amen". Even if we don't always understand the timing, He always finishes what He starts.

Rejoice today knowing that He has made promises over your life, and He will complete every one of them.

Scripture:

"For all of God's promises have been fulfilled in Christ with a resounding 'Yes!' And through Christ, our 'Amen' (which means 'Yes') ascends to God for His glory."

2 Corinthians 1:20 NLT

Activation:

Reflect on the promises that God has spoken over your life. Thank Him for the promises He has made and trust Him to fulfill every one that He has made to you.

God is Good All the Time!

Have you stopped and said the phrase, "God is good all the time"?

Let's say it together right now: God is good all the time!

God is good when I'm at school or working from home. God is good when I have to do chores. God is good when I am playing and having fun with my friends. God is good when it is raining. God is good when the sun is shining.

God is good all of the time. No matter what, all of the time, when I am happy, or when I am sad, God is good.

Saying these words helps push past our flesh when things are not always going the way we want them to go. When we can't see the full picture of what God is doing, reminding ourselves of the goodness of God takes away our limited thinking and trusts the Lord with the results. His big picture is more amazing than we can even imagine!

Activation:

Write down in your notebook areas where you can thank God that He is good. Writing down these truths will help remind you of His faithfulness on days that are hard and trust Him that the sun will shine again, even after the difficulties in your life.

Scripture:
"*The LORD is good to everyone. He showers compassion on all His creation.*"

Psalm 145:9 NLT

The Joy of the Lord Is Your Strength

The unspeakable joy of the Lord can fill your heart with gladness even in situations that are challenging. You can't explain what comes over you, but joy is a feeling that God can give you at all times when you trust in Jesus as your Lord and Savior.

When you feel weak, God is your strength.
If you have a hard test coming up, God can help you overcome your fear.
If people are saying mean things to you, God can remind you of your worth through the Holy Spirit and the reading of His Word.
If you feel alone, God can remind you that He is always there.

In every moment, you can know that God has a purpose for your life. You can have peace knowing that you are seen, loved, valued, chosen, and that God's plans are always for your good and His glory.

Have joy in all circumstances, knowing that you are God's incredible creation, and He sees you right where you are and loves you.

Activation:

Pray and ask the Lord to show you someone in your life to encourage with your words or actions. Encouraging others can bring your heart great joy.

P

You Will Reap a Harvest

Fall signals harvest season, and Pete the Puzzle Piece goes to the pumpkin patch in the town of Jigsaw at this time and reminds himself that God brings the harvest.

Farmers spend countless hours working their fields and tending to their crops. Their efforts are not in vain. In the same way, you may spend hours working and doing things that God has entrusted to you, and you will see the rewards for your efforts in due time.

Do all God has called you to do with excellence, and watch Him crown your efforts with success.

Pete the Puzzle Piece is cheering for you as you faithfully continue doing your work well. Most of all, the Heavenly Father is cheering you on and giving you encouragement to not grow weary in doing good. He knows how to reward you with the harvest at just the right time.

Activation:

If possible in your area, ask parental or guardian permission to visit a farm nearby, whether it be sunflowers or a pumpkin patch and visualize the harvest. Draw what you see. See the rewards of the farmer's efforts in real time.

God Crowns the Year with His Goodness

What does it mean to "Crown your year"? It can refer to your year being special because you are having victorious success.

Wow! The Bible talks about how God is able to crown our year with victory and with His goodness. I want that! Don't you?

Harvest time reminds us all to ask God and believe for Him to crown our efforts and our year with His supernatural success.

He can cause our lives to overflow with His abundance so that we can be a blessing to others...Not for us to brag but to help others and to show the greatness of the Heavenly Father.

When God blesses us, we can show how thankful we are by being a blessing to others.

Activation:

Write the above Scripture passage in your notebook. Pray and ask God how you can be a blessing to those around you. Look for ways as the Lord leads you to be a blessing.

J.O.Y.

What can you do to experience "JOY"?
Some people remind themselves with J.O.Y.

First, prioritize Jesus in your life. Seek Him first in all you do, and He will direct your steps. Keeping Him first puts everything else in the right order in your life.

Second, prioritize others. As you bless others around you, you become less focused on yourself. One smile or one word of encouragement that God leads you to share with someone else could change their life forever. Let's make sure we are always speaking the truth in love and showing kindness with our words and actions. If you need to ask someone for forgiveness, today is a great day to do that.

Third, think of yourself. Notice that this is the last item in the J.O.Y. Taking care of yourself is important. Your body is the temple of the Holy Spirit. It is important to get rest, eat a balanced diet, exercise, and have time to recharge by spending time with the Lord.
When we combine all of these, it helps keep our priorities on the right track no matter the season.
May your heart be filled with JOY always.

Activation:

On a 3x5 or 4x6 notecard write J.O.Y. and with parental or guardian permission, put that notecard on the refrigerator or bathroom mirror to remind yourself to prioritize Jesus. Others. Yourself in that order.

Scripture:

"May He grant your heart's desires and make all your plans succeed. May we shout for joy when we hear of your victory and raise a victory banner in the name of our God. May the LORD answer all your prayers."

Psalm 20:4-5 NLT

P

Fall in Love with Jesus

As the leaves fall from the trees, Pete the Puzzle Piece and Bobo the dog love to play in a giant leaf pile in Pete's backyard. Leaves of all colors—yellows, browns, reds, and orange hues surround them as they laugh and remind themselves of the goodness of God. One by one, they pick up a leaf and name a quality of God that comes to mind.

Faithful. Trustworthy. Loving, Just. Kind. Merciful. Longsuffering. Truthful. Good. All powerful.

There are so many incredible qualities of God to name!

As you look at the leaves falling from the trees, may they remind you to fall in love with Jesus by spending time with Him, thinking about His goodness, and growing your friendship with Him.

Activation:

Ask a parent or guardian to walk outside and collect some leaves. As you look at each one, think about a quality of God that encourages you. Write that quality down on a piece of paper or construction paper and tape the leaf above it. Place it on your refrigerator or mirror to remind yourself of the character of God.

Scripture:

"They know the truth about God because He has made it obvious to them. For ever since the world was created, people have seen the earth and sky. Through everything God made, they can clearly see His invisible qualities—His eternal power and Divine nature. So they have no excuse for not knowing God."

Romans 1:19-20 NLT

Count Your Blessings

At this time of year, Pete the Puzzle Piece and his pals gather together and count their blessings. As they sit at the table and eat, they share what they are thankful for with one another. They have a jar that they pass around, and in the jar they place a sheet of paper, and each one puts a sheet of paper in the jar with something that they are counting as a blessing this year.

Pete encourages you to do the same. Start thinking and remembering blessings this year. As you begin to think of some, write them down on a sheet of paper. You can fold the sheet of paper and place it in a jar or container. This time next year, you can read them aloud with your friends and family.

What a great reminder to record and share your blessings throughout the year!

Activation:

Ask a parent or guardian permission to use a jar or container in your house to begin the "Counting Your Blessings" jar. As you remember a blessing throughout the year, write it on a sheet of paper, fold it, and put it in the jar. A year from now, sit at the table and read the words aloud to recount the blessings God has done.

Scripture:

"Let all that I am praise the LORD; may I never forget the good things He does for me. He forgives all my sins and heals all my diseases. He redeems me from death and crowns me with love and tender mercies. He fills my life with good things. My youth is renewed like the eagle's!"

Psalm 103:2-5 NLT

Give Thanks in All Circumstances

When was the last time you told someone, "Thank you"? One simple phrase can mean so much. When you stop and think about what you are thankful for, what are some that you can name?

Stop right now and try to name some aloud.

There is so much to be thankful for in this life even on the hard days. As you focus on thankfulness, it can remind you that the difficulties that you are facing will eventually pass, and the sun will shine again. If you haven't told someone, "Thank you" recently, now would be a good time to say it. Think about people in your life who work hard to make sure you are taken care of, the teacher who teaches you, or the friend who makes you laugh or listens. Thank Jesus for all that He has done through His sacrifice on the cross and His resurrection.

Think about people you don't normally thank that might be overlooked and could use a word of kindness.

This time of year reminds us to give thanks in all circumstances.

Activation:

Write someone a "Thank you" card. Take the time to share with them why you are thankful. When you hand it to them, it is a wonderful opportunity to brighten someone's day and let them know how special they are in your life.

Love Came Down

During the winter months, Pete the Puzzle Piece sits on the park bench and reflects on the upcoming celebration of Jesus' birth. It is such a special time remembering that God is a miracle worker and that He humbled Himself to come to this earth to save mankind.

Jesus was born in simple circumstances in a stable with farm animals. He came so that we might live. He is the ultimate example of humility. Humility means that you consider others more important than yourself. It also means that you are not being proud or arrogant.

As Pete sits on the park bench, he remembers that Jesus chose us over comfort. The King of the world was born in a manger. What a powerful symbol to humble ourselves with others. The greatest example of love, Jesus, reminds us all to do justly, to love mercy, and to walk humbly with one another.

Activation:

Read Luke 2:1-20 aloud with a parent or guardian. Talk about how Jesus came to earth and what stands out to you from reading about the Nativity.

Scripture:

"No, O people, the LORD has told you what is good, and this is what He requires of you: to do what is right, to love mercy, and to walk humbly with your God."

Micah 6:8 NLT

Park Bench Moments

Park Bench moments are times to sit and reflect on the year as a new one is about to begin.

Questions that you answer about yourself in the quiet and stillness as you sit and think:

1. What have I learned about myself this year?
2. In what areas have I grown?
3. In what areas do I want to develop myself in this upcoming year?
4. What lies or comparison about myself did I ask the Lord to help me overcome?
5. What does God say about me as His special creation?
6. How can I bring joy into the life of someone else?
7. Do I believe what God says about me?
8. How do I share God's love with the world around me?

Activation:

Write in your journal or notebook the questions that are listed above. As you sit and think about these questions, write down the answers.

Scripture:

"Let all that I am wait quietly before God, for my hope is in Him."

Psalm 62:5 NLT

The Greatest Gift

What is the greatest gift that you have ever received? What made it so special?

Have you thought about the fact that Jesus is the greatest gift? This time of year is a wonderful remembrance of His birth. Many give gifts to one another during this season. As you give and receive gifts, remember that since Jesus is our greatest gift, He gives us gifts to share with the world.

You are created on purpose for a purpose to do the special things that God planned for you long ago. As you get ready to begin a new year, walk with confidence into all that He has planned for you.

The Savior of the world is right there to give you the courage to fulfill all the things that He has called you to do for His honor and glory. As the greatest gift, Jesus loves to see you sharing the giftings He has given you with others.

Activation:

As a gift to your loved ones, decorate 3x5 or 4x6 cards, and write special things about them on the card. Once you are finished designing the cards, hand it to them to show how much you appreciate and value them. Since you are so special, you also recognize how important those God placed in your life are, too.

THE PETE ADVENTURE SERIES & ACTIVITY BOOKS

I AM SPECIAL DEVOTIONAL *BUNDLE

Purchase the I Am Special Interactive Journal as a companion to the I Am Special Devotional in this special bundle offer.

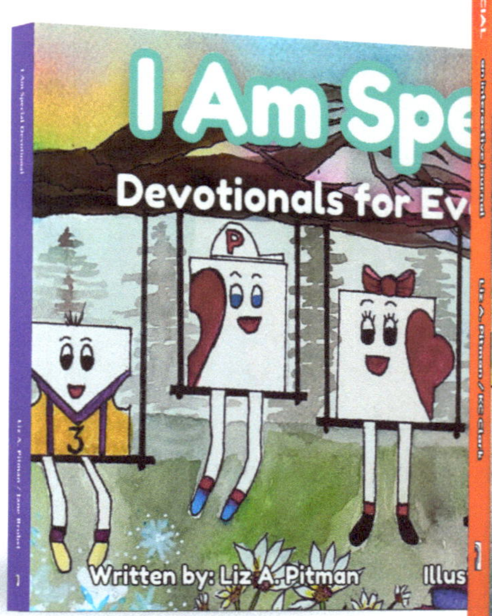

9 798986 888996